# A.1. STEAK SAUCE

# GREAT GRILLING

PUBLICATIONS INTERNATIONAL, LTD.

**Copyright © 1995 Nabisco, Inc.**
All rights reserved.

A.1. is a registered trademark of Nabisco, Inc.

All recipes kitchen tested in NABISCO FOODS GROUP CONSUMER FOOD CENTER.

This edition published by Publications International, Ltd.,
7373 N. Cicero Ave., Lincolnwood, IL 60646.

**Photography:** Sacco Productions Limited, Chicago

**Pictured on the front cover:** *(top to bottom)*: Barbecue Ribettes *(page 18),* A.1. Dry Spice Rub *(page 38)* and South-of-the-Border Vegetable Kabobs *(page 56).*

**Pictured on the back cover** *(clockwise from top left)*: Skillet Steak Fajitas *(page 84),* Sunshine Chicken Drumsticks *(page 14),* America's Favorite Cheddar Beef Burgers *(page 66)* and Grilled Beef 'n' Vegetable-Topped Pizza *(page 74).*

ISBN: 0-7853-1182-3

Manufactured in U.S.A.

8 7 6 5 4 3 2 1

INTRODUCTION                         6

APPETIZERS                          10

MARINADES, SAUCES AND BASTES        24

SIZZLING STEAKS                     34

BEYOND BEEF                         52

BURGER BASICS                       62

GRILL CRAZY                         72

RAINY DAY FAVORITES                 84

INDEX                               93

# Introduction

## A.1.®, HOW GRILLING IS DONE

If the sound of meat sizzling over hot coals and the rich, smoky aroma of grilled food excite your appetite, these A.1.® grill recipes are just what you need.

Whether you're in the mood for a thick, juicy T-bone, a big, hearty burger or a tender piece of grilled chicken, A.1.® Steak Sauce and its spicier counterpart, A.1.® Bold, are the perfect grilling ingredients. Both sauces have just the right mix of herbs and spices to blend with the meat's natural juices and transform you into a true grillmaster.

**THE GRILL:** There are many different grills, from a simple hibachi to a super deluxe gas grill that monitors internal meat temperatures. We at A.1. do not recommend or require any particular type of grill for our recipes. If you have your choice, however, the larger models provide more flexibility to move food around to hotter and cooler spots on the grill. Recently, gas grills have become very popular. If you own a gas grill, and desire more information, we recommend that you consult your owner's manual for specifics on your particular grill.

**THE FUEL:** There are four basic types of fuel: (1) propane gas, (2) charcoal briquettes, (3) hardwood lump charcoal and (4) hardwood itself. Propane gas is very convenient and provides instant heat. For slower cooking foods, however, it provides less of a smoky flavor than charcoal. For charcoal-burning grills, standard charcoal briquettes found in grocery stores are an adequate fuel. Many will argue that hardwood lump charcoal is the best fuel because it contains no additives, starts easily, burns cleanly and lasts a long time. Hardwood is also acceptable, but it is difficult to control, burns irregularly and requires a long precooking start-up time.

**THE FUEL BED:** Spread out plenty of coals to create a large cooking area on which to grill your food to perfection. Make a charcoal bed about four inches thick and slightly larger than the surface area of the item you are about to grill; outline that area with a ring of briquettes about two inches high. This approach gives adequate room to manipulate food on the grill during the cooking process.

**STARTING THE FIRE:** Convenience is important as long as you do not interfere with the taste of the food. For this reason, you should avoid using presoaked charcoal briquettes since they are soaked with lighter fluid and release chemical fumes throughout the cooking process. Lighter fluid sprinkled on charcoal briquettes just before lighting, however, is perfectly acceptable. Contrary to popular opinion, it does not give an unpleasant taste to the food because it burns off within the first five to ten minutes. After piling your briquettes, liberally apply lighter fluid and allow it to soak in for several minutes before igniting.

**TIME TO START COOKING:** Gas grills are ready to cook on just minutes after lighting. For charcoal-burning grills, you must wait for the flames to die since it is preferable to cook over coals rather than flames. Start grilling when the coals have a uniform gray ash coating. This coating usually forms after about 30 to 40 minutes for a hot fire, 40 to 45 minutes for a medium fire (we recommend a medium fire for most of our recipes) and 45 to 50 minutes for a low fire. Remember, these times are approximate and can be affected by weather, altitude, covering of the grill, and the distance of the cooking rack from the fire.

**PREPARING THE GRILL:** Just before placing food on the grill, lightly brush the hot cooking rack with oil to reduce sticking of the food. Use a long-handled basting brush since oil drips can cause flare-ups. We also recommend cleaning your grill with a wire brush before each use. Contrary to popular belief, black build-up on the cooking rack does not add to the smoky flavor of the food; it simply encourages the food to stick.

**FLARE-UPS:** While dripping juices and fats give the food a pleasant smoky flavor, they can also cause flare-ups and result in overly charred food. Trimming excess fat from your food before grilling will help reduce flare-ups. If a flare-up does occur, a spray bottle filled with water is a useful tool. Set the sprayer on "stream" and aim directly for the spot where the fat is dripping onto the coals. If this doesn't work, cover the grill and close the vents halfway to cool the fire. If flare-ups are still a problem, your fire is too hot. Remove your food, close the vents completely, cover the grill, and wait 5 to 10 minutes before putting your food back on.

**OPEN OR COVERED:** If your grill is open, the coals will tend to be hotter and prone to flare-ups. The food will cook quickly on the outside, sealing the juices in on the inside. As a general rule, if the food is less than 1½ inches thick and will cook sufficiently on the inside before burning on the outside, it is suitable for open grilling. Covering your grill prevents oxygen from flaming the coals and allows the heat to circulate around your food, cooking it more evenly. Foods that are more than 1½ inches thick or are fatty should be cooked on a covered grill.

**TESTING FOR DONENESS:** The charts on page 5 are guides for approximate grilling times. Remember, the thickness of the meat is important to consider for cooking time since the thicker the meat is, the longer it will take to cook.

Keep in mind that no two fires are the same. To ensure that the meat is grilled to your satisfaction, begin testing for doneness three to four minutes before the end of the cooking time listed on the chart. Although we do not recommend cutting the meat to determine doneness because it lets the juices escape, this method does eliminate guesswork. Remember that the meat will continue to cook for a few minutes after you remove it from the grill.

**SELECTING THE PROPER MEAT CUTS FOR GRILLING**
In general, foods to be grilled should be relatively small in size and weight to properly cook on the inside before burning on the outside.

**Beef:** Since grilling is quick, dry-heat cooking, tender cuts of beef are best; purchase cuts labeled "prime" or "choice". Look for bright red, firm meat with marbling, which provides an internal basting liquid. Never add salt to beef before or during grilling as it draws out the juices that make beef tender.

**Veal:** Rib and loin cuts of veal are best suited for the grill. Because veal is low in fat, it cooks very quickly.

**Lamb:** The best cuts for grilling include the loin, rib and leg of lamb, either boneless butterflied or bone-in.

**Pork:** The pork loin, particularly the center cut, is the most tender and therefore best for the grill. Boned pork loin roasts are also superb when marinated and grilled. Pork ribs, including country-style, baby back and spare ribs, are grill favorites.

**Chicken:** All chicken parts are suitable for grilling. Boneless chicken is great for quick meals because it has the smaller mass necessary for fast grilling.

**Fish:** The best types of fish to grill are those sold as steaks, such as tuna, salmon, and swordfish. Because of their thickness, they are easier to turn and less likely to fall apart. More delicate whole fish or fillets are best grilled in a rotisserie basket.

**RECIPE NOTATIONS**

Indicates recipes that use A.1.® Bold Steak Sauce.

Indicates recipes that are prepared from start to finish in 30 minutes or less.

**LET THE GRILLING BEGIN:** Now that we have shared with you some of the basics on grilling, you are ready to sample our delicious recipes and discover why we say, A.1.®, How Grilling is Done!

## Grilling Chart

| Meat, Poultry & Fish | Total Time Minutes (over medium heat) |
|---|---|
| Beef Top Round Steak (¾ to 1 inch thick) | 12 to 14 |
| Beef Sirloin, T-Bone, Shell, Strip, Rib-Eye Steaks (¾ inch thick) | 8 to 11 |
| Beef Flank Steak (1½ pounds) | 8 to 10 |
| Beef Kabobs (¾-inch cubes) | 4 to 6 |
| Beef Kabobs (1 to 1½-inch cubes) | 8 to 10 |
| Ground Beef Patties (¾ inch thick) | 8 to 12 |
| Ground Beef Patties (1 inch thick) | 12 to 16 |
| Pork Chops (1 inch thick) | 15 to 20 |
| Boneless Chicken Breast Halves (4 ounces) | 6 to 8 |
| Whole Chicken, cut up into 8 pieces | 30 to 45 |
| Fish, Fillets or Steaks | 10 to 12 per pound |

## Internal Temperature Chart

| Meat & Poultry | Doneness | Temperature |
|---|---|---|
| Beef | Rare | 140°F |
| Beef | Medium | 160°F |
| Beef | Well-Done | 170°F |
| Pork | | 160°F |
| Chicken (Boneless) | | 165°F |
| Chicken (Bone-in) | | 180°F |

**A.1.**
**STEAK SAUCE**

# Appetizers

## GRILLED ANTIPASTO

⅔ **cup A.1. Steak Sauce**
¼ **cup lemon juice**
2 **tablespoons olive oil**
1 **teaspoon dried basil leaves**
2 **cloves garlic, minced**
16 **medium scallops (about ⅔ pound)**
16 **medium shrimp, shelled and deveined (about ¾ pound)**
12 **mushrooms**
2 **ounces thinly sliced cooked roast beef or ham**
16 **(2×½-inch) eggplant strips**
1 **(6½-ounce) jar marinated artichoke hearts, drained**
1 **red bell pepper, thickly sliced**
   **Lettuce leaves and lemon wedges, for garnish**

Soak 12 (10-inch) wooden skewers in water for at least 30 minutes. In medium bowl, combine steak sauce, lemon juice, olive oil, basil and garlic; set aside.

Thread 4 scallops onto each of 4 skewers and 4 shrimp onto each of 4 skewers; thread 6 mushrooms onto each of 2 skewers. Cut roast beef or ham into 3×1-inch strips; wrap around eggplant strips and secure with wooden toothpick. Wrap remaining beef or ham around artichoke hearts; thread onto remaining 2 skewers. Place skewers, eggplant bundles and pepper slices on baking sheet; brush with steak sauce mixture.

Grill over medium heat for 7 to 10 minutes or until seafood is opaque and vegetables are tender, turning and basting several times. Remove each item from grill as it is done; place on large lettuce-lined serving platter. Serve garnished with lemon wedges if desired.

*Makes 8 appetizer servings*

# COWBOY KABOBS

⅓ **cup A.1. Steak Sauce**
⅓ **cup barbecue sauce**
2 **teaspoons prepared horseradish**
1 **(1½-pound) beef top round steak, cut into ½-inch strips**
8 **pearl onions**
8 **bell pepper strips**

Soak 16 (10-inch) wooden skewers in water for at least 30 minutes. In small bowl, combine steak sauce, barbecue sauce and horseradish; set aside.

Thread steak strips onto skewers; place one onion or pepper strip on end of each skewer. Place kabobs in glass dish; coat with steak sauce mixture. Cover; chill 1 hour, turning occasionally. Grill kabobs over medium heat for 4 to 6 minutes or until done, turning occasionally. Serve hot.

*Makes 16 appetizers*

# FIESTA CHICKEN WINGS

1 **cup A.1. Steak Sauce**
1 **cup mild, medium or hot thick and chunky salsa**
10 **chicken wings, split and tips removed**

In medium bowl, combine steak sauce and salsa; reserve 1 cup for dipping.

In nonmetal bowl, coat wings with remaining sauce. Cover; chill 1 hour, turning occasionally. Grill wings over medium heat for 12 to 15 minutes or until no longer pink, turning occasionally. Serve hot with reserved sauce.

*Makes 20 appetizers*

# A.1. VIRGIN MARY

2 **cups tomato juice**
3 **tablespoons A.1. Steak Sauce**
¼ **to ½ teaspoon liquid hot pepper seasoning, optional**
**Ice cubes**
4 **lime or lemon wedges, for garnish**
4 **celery stalks, for garnish**

In small pitcher, blend tomato juice, steak sauce and hot pepper seasoning. Pour into 4 ice-filled 8-ounce glasses. Garnish with lime or lemon wedges and celery stalks. Serve immediately.

*Makes 4 servings*

## SUNSHINE CHICKEN DRUMSTICKS

½ cup A.1. Steak Sauce
¼ cup ketchup
¼ cup apricot preserves
12 chicken drumsticks (about 2½ pounds)

In small bowl, using wire whisk, blend steak sauce, ketchup and preserves until smooth. Brush chicken with sauce.

Grill chicken over medium heat for 20 minutes or until done, turning and brushing with remaining sauce. Serve hot.          *Makes 12 appetizers*

## HOT BLUE CHEESE DIP WITH GRILLED VEGETABLES

2 tablespoons margarine
2 tablespoons all-purpose flour
1½ cups milk
¾ cup A.1. Steak Sauce
⅓ cup crumbled blue cheese (about 1½ ounces)
1 medium eggplant, quartered lengthwise and cut into
    ½-inch-thick slices
2 small zucchini, cut into ½-inch rounds
12 medium mushrooms (about 4 ounces)
8 green onions, cut into 2-inch pieces
2 small red bell peppers, cut into 1-inch strips
2 tablespoons olive oil

Soak 12 (10-inch) wooden skewers in water for at least 30 minutes. In medium saucepan, over medium heat, melt margarine. Stir in flour; cook for 1 minute. Gradually stir in milk; cook and stir until mixture thickens and begins to boil. Stir in ½ cup steak sauce and cheese; heat until cheese melts. Keep cheese dip warm.

Alternately thread vegetables onto skewers. Combine remaining steak sauce and oil. Grill vegetables over medium heat for 8 to 10 minutes or until done, turning and brushing with steak sauce/oil mixture. Serve warm with warm cheese dip.          *Makes 12 appetizer servings*

## SURF AND TURF BROCHETTES

  1 (12-ounce) beef top round steak, cut into ¾-inch cubes
24 small shrimp, peeled and deveined
  1 green bell pepper, cut into 1-inch squares
¾ cup orange juice
½ cup A.1. Steak Sauce
  2 tablespoons white wine
  1 clove garlic, minced
1½ teaspoons cornstarch

Soak 12 (10-inch) wooden skewers in water for at least 30 minutes. Alternately thread beef cubes, shrimp and green pepper onto skewers.

In small saucepan, combine orange juice, steak sauce, wine and garlic; reserve ½ cup mixture for basting. Blend cornstarch into remaining steak sauce mixture in saucepan. Over medium heat, cook and stir until sauce thickens and begins to boil; keep warm.

Grill brochettes over medium heat for 8 to 10 minutes or until done, turning and brushing often with reserved steak sauce mixture. Serve brochettes with warm sauce for dipping. *Makes 12 appetizers*

## ASIAN BEEF BITES

½ cup A.1. BOLD Steak Sauce
  2 tablespoons dry sherry
  1 tablespoon peanut oil
  1 tablespoon sesame oil
  1 tablespoon toasted sesame seed
  1 clove garlic, minced
  1 teaspoon minced fresh ginger
  1 pound beef top round steak, cut into ¾-inch cubes
18 snow peas, halved crosswise

Soak 18 (10-inch) wooden skewers in water for at least 30 minutes. In small bowl, combine steak sauce, sherry, peanut and sesame oils, sesame seed, garlic and ginger; set aside.

Thread beef cubes onto skewers, ending with a snow pea half; place in glass dish. Pour marinade over skewers, coating completely. Cover; chill 1 hour, turning occasionally. Grill over medium heat for 4 to 6 minutes or until done, turning and brushing often with marinade. Serve hot.

*Makes 1½ dozen appetizers*

## GREEK GRILLED PIZZA WEDGES

⅓ **cup prepared pizza sauce**
¼ **cup A.1. Steak Sauce**
4 **(6-inch) whole wheat pita breads**
2 **tablespoons olive oil**
4 **ounces deli sliced roast beef, coarsely chopped**
½ **cup chopped tomato**
⅓ **cup sliced pitted ripe olives**
½ **cup crumbled feta cheese\* (2 ounces)**

In small bowl, combine pizza sauce and steak sauce; set aside. Brush both sides of pita bread with oil. Spread sauce mixture on one side of each pita; top with roast beef, tomato, olives and feta cheese.

Grill prepared pita, topping side up, over medium heat for 4 to 5 minutes or until topping is hot and pita is crisp. Cut each pita into 4 wedges to serve.
*Makes 8 appetizer servings*

\*¾ cup shredded mozzarella cheese may be substituted.

## BARBECUE RIBETTES

1 **clove garlic, minced**
1 **tablespoon vegetable oil**
½ **cup ketchup**
⅓ **cup A.1. Steak Sauce**
¼ **cup chili sauce**
2 **tablespoons firmly packed light brown sugar**
2 **thin slices fresh lemon**
½ **teaspoon liquid hot pepper seasoning**
2½ **pounds pork baby back ribs, split**

In medium saucepan, over low heat, cook garlic in oil until tender. Stir in ketchup, steak sauce, chili sauce, brown sugar, lemon slices and hot pepper seasoning; simmer 1 to 2 minutes or until heated through.

Arrange ribs on rack in large roasting pan. Bake at 400°F for 30 minutes. Brush ribs generously with prepared sauce. Grill over medium heat for 20 to 25 minutes or until done, turning and brushing often with remaining sauce. Slice into individual ribs to serve. *Makes 8 appetizer servings*

## ALMOND CHICKEN KABOBS

⅓ cup A.1. BOLD Steak Sauce
1 tablespoon Dijon mustard
1 tablespoon honey
1 tablespoon vegetable oil
1 tablespoon lemon juice
1 clove garlic, crushed
4 boneless chicken breast halves (about 1 pound)
¼ cup toasted slivered almonds, chopped

In small bowl, combine steak sauce, mustard, honey, oil, lemon juice and garlic; set aside.

Cut each chicken breast half into 8 cubes. In medium nonmetal bowl, combine chicken cubes and ½ cup steak sauce mixture. Cover; chill 1 hour, turning occasionally.

Soak 16 (10-inch) wooden skewers in water for at least 30 minutes. Thread 2 chicken cubes onto each skewer. Grill kabobs over medium heat for 6 to 8 minutes or until done, turning and brushing with remaining sauce. Remove from grill; quickly roll kabobs in almonds. Serve immediately.

*Makes 16 appetizers*

## BEEFY NACHOS

1 pound ground beef
¼ cup chopped onion
⅓ cup A.1. Steak Sauce
5 cups tortilla chips
1 cup shredded Monterey Jack cheese (4 ounces)
  Dairy sour cream, optional
1 cup chopped tomato, optional
¼ cup diced green chiles, optional
¼ cup sliced pitted ripe olives, optional

In large skillet, over medium-high heat, brown beef and onion; drain. Stir in steak sauce. Arrange tortilla chips on large heatproof platter. Spoon beef mixture over chips; sprinkle with cheese. Broil 6 inches from heat source for 3 to 5 minutes or until cheese melts. Top with sour cream, tomato, chiles and olives if desired. Serve immediately.

*Makes 6 appetizer servings*

# GRILLED FRUIT KABOBS

⅓ **cup dairy sour cream**
⅓ **cup apricot preserves**
¼ **cup A.1. Steak Sauce**
1½ **cups pineapple chunks (fresh or canned)**
  1 **cup seedless grapes**
  1 **orange, sectioned**
  1 **large banana, cut into 12 chunks**
  1 **tablespoon margarine, melted**

Soak 12 (10-inch) wooden skewers in water for at least 30 minutes. In small bowl, combine sour cream, apricot preserves and 1 tablespoon steak sauce; set aside.

Thread fruit pieces onto skewers. In small bowl, combine remaining 3 tablespoons steak sauce with melted margarine; brush kabobs with margarine mixture. Grill fruit over medium heat for 5 minutes or until warm and very lightly browned, turning and basting with remaining margarine mixture. Serve warm with sour cream sauce for dipping.

*Makes 12 appetizers*


# THAI CHICKEN RIBBONS

½ **cup A.1. Steak Sauce**
½ **cup creamy peanut butter**
¼ **cup water**
  2 **tablespoons reduced sodium soy sauce**
  2 **cloves garlic, minced**
  2 **tablespoons lime juice**
  2 **tablespoons firmly packed light brown sugar**
½ **teaspoon minced fresh ginger**
½ **teaspoon red pepper flakes**
1¼ **pounds boneless chicken breasts, cut lengthwise into**
      ½**-inch-wide strips**
  **Green onion brushes, for garnish**

Soak 12 (10-inch) wooden skewers in water for at least 30 minutes. In small saucepan, combine steak sauce, peanut butter, water, soy sauce, garlic, lime juice, brown sugar, ginger and red pepper. Over medium heat, cook and stir for 2 to 3 minutes or until smooth.

Thread chicken strips onto skewers. Reserve 1 cup sauce and keep warm for dipping. Grill chicken over medium heat for 6 to 8 minutes or until done, turning and brushing with remaining sauce. Remove from grill; garnish with onion brushes. Serve hot with reserved sauce for dipping.

*Makes 12 appetizers*

# Marinades, Sauces and Bastes

## THAI MARINADE

**½ cup A.1. Steak Sauce**
**⅓ cup peanut butter**
**2 tablespoons soy sauce**

In small nonmetal bowl, combine steak sauce, peanut butter and soy sauce. Use to marinate beef, poultry or pork for about 1 hour in the refrigerator.                                    *Makes 1 cup*

## PEPPER TRIO SAUCE

**1 cup chopped onion**
**2 tablespoons margarine**
**1 cup *each* red, green and yellow bell pepper strips**
**½ cup A.1. Steak Sauce**
**½ cup prepared spaghetti sauce**
**½ cup chopped tomato**

In large skillet, over medium-high heat, cook onion in margarine until slightly tender. Add peppers; cook and stir until tender-crisp, about 5 minutes. Add steak sauce, spaghetti sauce and tomato; heat to a boil. Reduce heat; simmer 5 minutes. Serve warm with cooked beef, poultry or pork.                                    *Makes 3 cups*

## HONEY BASTING SAUCE

**¾ cup A.1. Steak Sauce**
**2 tablespoons honey**
**2 tablespoons dry sherry**
**1 teaspoon cornstarch**
**¼ teaspoon dried basil leaves**

In small saucepan, blend steak sauce, honey, sherry, cornstarch and basil. Over medium heat, heat to a boil, stirring constantly. Boil 1 minute; remove from heat and cool slightly. Use as a baste while grilling beef, poultry or pork.      *Makes about 1 cup*

## LEMON PEPPER MARINADE

**⅔ cup A.1. Steak Sauce**
**4 teaspoons grated lemon peel**
**1½ teaspoons coarsely ground black pepper**

In small nonmetal bowl, combine steak sauce, lemon peel and pepper. Use to marinate beef, fish steak, poultry or pork for about 1 hour in the refrigerator.      *Makes about ⅔ cup*

## QUICK BARBECUE BASTING SAUCE

**½ cup A.1. Steak Sauce**
**½ cup ketchup**
**½ teaspoon liquid hot pepper seasoning**

In small bowl, combine steak sauce, ketchup and hot pepper seasoning. Use as a baste while grilling beef, ribs or poultry.      *Makes 1 cup*

## TERIYAKI MARINADE

**½ cup A.1. Steak Sauce**
**¼ cup teriyaki sauce**
**2 tablespoons Dijon mustard**

In small nonmetal bowl, combine steak sauce, teriyaki sauce and mustard. Use to marinate beef, fish steak, poultry or pork for about 1 hour in the refrigerator.      *Makes ¾ cup*

# TANGY LEMON GLAZE

½ **cup apple juice**
¼ **cup firmly packed light brown sugar**
½ **cup A.1. Steak Sauce**
2 **tablespoons lemon juice**
1 **tablespoon cornstarch**
1 **teaspoon grated lemon peel**

In small saucepan, blend apple juice and brown sugar. Stir in steak sauce, lemon juice, cornstarch and lemon peel. Over medium heat, heat to a boil, stirring constantly. Boil 1 minute; remove from heat and cool slightly. Use as a baste while grilling poultry, pork or ham.      *Makes about 1¼ cups*

# BOLD MUSHROOM SAUCE

½ **cup sliced onion**
2 **tablespoons margarine**
1½ **cups sliced mushrooms**
¾ **cup A.1. BOLD Steak Sauce**

In medium skillet, over medium heat, sauté onion in margarine until tender, about 5 minutes. Stir in mushrooms; cook and stir 5 minutes more. Add steak sauce; heat to a boil. Reduce heat; simmer 5 minutes. Serve hot with cooked beef or pork.      *Makes 1½ cups*

# CHILI MARINADE

¼ **cup A.1. Steak Sauce**
¼ **cup chili sauce**

In small nonmetal bowl, combine steak sauce and chili sauce. Use to marinate beef or pork for about 1 hour in the refrigerator.

*Makes ½ cup*

# STEAK MARINADE PROVENÇALE

½ **cup A.1. Steak Sauce**
1½ **teaspoons coarsely ground black pepper**
2 **cloves garlic, crushed**

In small nonmetal bowl, combine steak sauce, black pepper and garlic. Use to marinate beef, poultry or pork for about 1 hour in the refrigerator.

*Makes ½ cup*

# MUSHROOM BACON SAUCE

**5 slices bacon, cut into ¼-inch pieces (about 4 ounces)**
**1 (10-ounce) package mushrooms, sliced (about 4 cups)**
**¼ cup A.1. Steak Sauce**
**2 tablespoons sherry cooking wine**

In large skillet, over medium-high heat, cook bacon until crisp. Remove bacon with slotted spoon. Reserve 2 tablespoons drippings.

In same skillet, sauté mushrooms in reserved drippings for 5 minutes or until tender. Stir in steak sauce, sherry and bacon; bring to a boil. Reduce heat; simmer 5 minutes. Serve hot with cooked beef, burgers or poultry.

*Makes 1½ cups*

# STEAK MARINADE ITALIANO

**¼ cup A.1. Steak Sauce**
**¼ cup prepared Italian salad dressing**
**1 teaspoon garlic powder**

In small nonmetal bowl, combine steak sauce, salad dressing and garlic powder. Use to marinate beef, poultry or pork for about 1 hour in the refrigerator.

*Makes ½ cup*

# ORANGE BARBECUE SAUCE

**¾ cup orange marmalade**
**½ cup A.1. BOLD Steak Sauce**
**½ cup Dijon mustard**
**¼ cup finely chopped onion**

In small bowl, combine marmalade, steak sauce, mustard and onion. Use as a baste while grilling poultry, ribs or pork.

*Makes about 2 cups*

## ONION WINE SAUCE

**4 cups onion wedges**
**2 cloves garlic, minced**
**2 tablespoons margarine**
**½ cup A.1. Steak Sauce**
**2 tablespoons red cooking wine**

In large skillet, over medium-high heat, cook and stir onions and garlic in margarine until tender, about 10 minutes. Stir in steak sauce and wine; heat to a boil. Reduce heat; simmer 5 minutes. Serve hot with cooked beef or poultry.      *Makes 2½ cups*

## CREAMY HORSERADISH SAUCE

**1 (8-ounce) package cream cheese, softened**
**⅓ cup A.1. Steak Sauce**
**3 tablespoons prepared horseradish, drained**
**2 tablespoons chopped green onion**

In medium bowl, blend cream cheese, steak sauce and horseradish; stir in onion. Cover; chill at least 1 hour or up to 2 days. Serve cold or at room temperature with cooked beef, sausage, fish or baked potatoes.      *Makes 1½ cups*

## BOLD PEPPER SAUCE

**1 cup thinly sliced red bell pepper**
**1 cup thinly sliced green bell pepper**
**2 tablespoons margarine**
**¾ cup A.1. BOLD Steak Sauce**
**1 tablespoon dry sherry**

In medium skillet, over medium-high heat, sauté peppers in margarine until tender-crisp, about 5 minutes. Stir in steak sauce and sherry; heat to a boil. Reduce heat; simmer 5 minutes. Serve warm with cooked beef or poultry.      *Makes 1¾ cups*

# CURRIED BARBECUE SAUCE

¼ **cup chopped green onions**
1 **clove garlic, crushed**
1 **tablespoon vegetable oil**
1 **teaspoon curry powder**
⅓ **cup Dijon mustard**
⅓ **cup A.1. Steak Sauce**
½ **cup plain lowfat yogurt**

In small saucepan, over low heat, cook onions and garlic in oil until tender, stirring frequently. Stir in curry powder; cook 1 minute. Stir in mustard and steak sauce. Remove saucepan from heat; cool slightly. Stir in yogurt. Use as a baste while grilling poultry, lamb or pork. *Makes about 1⅓ cups*

# TANGY MARMALADE MARINADE

⅓ **cup A.1. Steak Sauce**
¼ **cup ketchup**
¼ **cup orange marmalade**
2 **tablespoons lemon juice**

In small nonmetal bowl, combine steak sauce, ketchup, marmalade and lemon juice. Use to marinate beef, poultry or pork for about 1 hour in the refrigerator. *Makes about 1 cup*

# GLAZED ONION SAUCE

4 **cups thinly sliced Spanish onions, cut into 1-inch pieces**
½ **cup A.1. Steak Sauce**
⅓ **cup firmly packed light brown sugar**
½ **cup beef broth**

In heavy skillet, over medium-high heat, heat onions, steak sauce, brown sugar and beef broth to a boil. Reduce heat; simmer for 25 to 30 minutes, stirring occasionally or until onions are glazed and syrupy. Serve hot or at room temperature with cooked beef, burgers, poultry or pork. *Makes 2 cups*

**A.1.**
**STEAK**
**SAUCE**

# Sizzling Steaks

## ZESTY LEMON-GLAZED STEAK

⅓ cup A.1. Steak Sauce
2 teaspoons grated lemon peel
1 clove garlic, minced
¼ teaspoon coarsely ground black pepper
¼ teaspoon dried oregano leaves
4 (4- to 6-ounce) beef shell or strip steaks, about 1 inch thick

In small bowl, combine steak sauce, lemon peel, garlic, pepper and oregano; brush on both sides of steaks. Grill steaks over medium heat for 5 minutes on each side or until done, brushing with sauce occasionally. Serve immediately. *Makes 4 servings*

## MEXICAN FLANK STEAK

½ cup A.1. Steak Sauce
1 (4-ounce) can diced green chiles
2 tablespoons lime juice*
1 (1½-pound) beef flank steak, lightly scored

In blender or food processor, blend steak sauce, chiles and lime juice until smooth. Place steak in glass dish; coat with ½ cup chile mixture. Cover; chill 1 hour, turning occasionally.

Remove steak from marinade; reserve marinade. Grill steak over medium heat for 6 minutes on each side or until done, brushing often with reserved marinade. Thinly slice steak to serve. *Makes 6 servings*

*Lemon juice may be substituted.

Zesty Lemon-Glazed Steak

# GAZPACHO STEAK ROLL

  1 (2-pound) beef flank steak, butterflied
⅔ cup A.1. Steak Sauce
  1 cup shredded Monterey Jack cheese (4 ounces)
½ cup chopped tomato
⅓ cup chopped cucumber
¼ cup chopped green pepper
  2 tablespoons sliced green onion

Open butterflied steak like a book on smooth surface and flatten slightly. Spread ⅓ cup steak sauce over surface. Layer remaining ingredients over sauce. Roll up steak from short edge; secure with wooden toothpicks or tie with string if necessary.

Grill steak roll over medium heat for 30 to 40 minutes or until done, turning and brushing often with remaining steak sauce during last 10 minutes of cooking. Remove toothpicks; slice and serve garnished as desired.

*Makes 8 servings*

# TIJUANA BLACKENED STEAK

¾ teaspoon garlic powder
¾ teaspoon onion powder
¾ teaspoon ground black pepper
½ teaspoon ground white pepper
¼ teaspoon ground red pepper
  4 (4- to 6-ounce) beef shell or strip steaks, about ½ inch thick
½ cup A.1. Steak Sauce
¼ cup margarine, melted

In small bowl, combine garlic powder, onion powder and peppers; spread on waxed paper. Coat both sides of steaks with seasoning mixture.

In small bowl, combine steak sauce and margarine. Grill steaks 10 to 15 minutes or until done, turning and brushing often with ¼ cup steak sauce mixture. Serve steaks with remaining steak sauce mixture.

*Makes 4 servings*

# A.1. DRY SPICE RUB

**1 tablespoon peppercorn mélange (black, white, green and pink)**
**1 teaspoon yellow mustard seed**
**1 teaspoon whole coriander seed**
**1 tablespoon firmly packed light brown sugar**
**2 cloves garlic, minced**
**1 (1½- to 2-pound) beef T-bone or sirloin steak**
**3 tablespoons A.1. BOLD Steak Sauce**

In food processor or spice grinder, combine peppercorns, mustard seed and coriander seed; process until coarsely crushed. Stir in brown sugar and garlic. Brush both sides of steak with steak sauce; sprinkle each side with spice mixture, pressing firmly into steak.

Grill steak over medium heat for 20 to 25 minutes or until done, turning occasionally. Serve with additional steak sauce if desired.

*Makes 6 servings*

# A.1. GRILLED FISH STEAKS

**1 pound salmon steaks or other fish steaks, about 1 inch thick**
**¼ cup A.1. Steak Sauce**
**1 tablespoon margarine, melted**
**½ teaspoon garlic powder**

Coat large sheet of aluminum foil with nonstick cooking spray; place fish steaks on foil. In small bowl, combine steak sauce, margarine and garlic powder; spoon over fish. Fold edges of foil together to seal; place seam side up on grill. Grill for about 10 minutes or until fish flakes easily when tested with fork. Carefully remove from grill. Serve immediately.

*Makes 4 servings*

# CITRUS GRILLED STEAK

  1 (6-ounce) can orange juice concentrate, thawed
½ cup A.1. Steak Sauce
¼ cup dry sherry
  1 clove garlic, minced
  2 (8-ounce) beef club or strip steaks, about 1 inch thick

In small bowl, combine orange juice concentrate, steak sauce, sherry and garlic. Place steaks in glass dish; coat with ½ cup orange juice mixture. Cover; chill 1 hour, turning occasionally.

In small saucepan, over medium heat, heat remaining orange juice mixture; keep warm.

Remove steaks from marinade. Grill over medium heat for 4 minutes on each side or until done, turning once. Serve steaks with reserved warm orange sauce.           *Makes 4 servings*

# HEARTY GRILLED TENDERLOINS

  2 cups sliced onions
  2 tablespoons margarine
  1 (8-ounce) can peeled tomatoes, drained and chopped
½ cup A.1. Steak Sauce
  2 tablespoons red wine vinegar
¼ cup chopped parsley
  4 (4- to 6-ounce) beef tenderloin steaks, about 1 inch thick

In medium saucepan, over medium-high heat, cook onions in margarine until tender. Add tomatoes, ¼ cup steak sauce and vinegar; heat to a boil. Reduce heat; simmer 5 minutes. Remove from heat; stir in parsley. Keep warm.

Grill steaks over medium heat for 5 minutes on each side or until done, brushing with remaining steak sauce. Serve steaks with warm sauce.
          *Makes 4 servings*

## TOURNEDOS WITH MUSHROOM WINE SAUCE

¼ **cup finely chopped shallots**
2 **tablespoons margarine**
¼ **pound small mushrooms, halved**
½ **cup A.1. Steak Sauce**
¼ **cup Burgundy or other dry red wine**
¼ **cup chopped parsley**
4 **(4-ounce) beef tenderloin steaks (tournedos), about 1 inch**
   **thick**

In medium saucepan, over medium heat, sauté shallots in margarine until tender. Stir in mushrooms; sauté 1 minute. Stir in steak sauce and wine; heat to a boil. Reduce heat; simmer for 10 minutes. Stir in parsley; keep warm.

Grill steaks over medium heat for 10 to 12 minutes or until done, turning occasionally. Serve steaks topped with warm sauce.          *Makes 4 servings*

## APRICOT-GLAZED HAM STEAKS

½ **cup A.1. BOLD Steak Sauce**
⅓ **cup apricot preserves**
¼ **cup firmly packed light brown sugar**
¼ **cup orange juice**
2 **(1-pound) fully cooked center-cut ham slices, ½ inch thick**
   **Orange slices and chopped parsley, for garnish**

In small bowl, combine steak sauce, apricot preserves, brown sugar and orange juice. Reserve ½ cup glaze.

In small saucepan, over medium heat, heat remaining glaze to a boil; keep warm.

Grill ham steaks over medium heat for 3 to 4 minutes on each side or until heated through, basting with reserved glaze. To serve, drizzle warm glaze over ham steaks; garnish with orange slices and parsley if desired.
                                            *Makes 6 to 8 servings*

## STEAK WITH HORSERADISH SAUCE

**4 ounces light cream cheese, softened**
**½ cup A.1. Steak Sauce**
**2 tablespoons prepared horseradish, drained**
**2 tablespoons chopped green onion**
**4 (4-ounce) beef shell or strip steaks, about 1 inch thick**

In small bowl, blend cream cheese, ¼ cup steak sauce and horseradish; stir in onion. Cover; chill until ready to serve.

Grill steaks over medium heat for 5 minutes on each side until done, turning once and brushing occasionally with remaining steak sauce. Serve steaks topped with horseradish sauce. *Makes 4 servings*

## GRILLED SAUERBRATEN STEAK

**½ cup A.1. Steak Sauce**
**½ cup dry red wine**
**1 (1½-pound) beef sirloin steak**
**½ cup water**
**2 tablespoons margarine**
**2 gingersnap cookies, finely rolled**

In small bowl, combine steak sauce and wine. Place steak in glass dish; coat with ½ cup steak sauce mixture. Cover; chill 1 hour, turning occasionally.

In small saucepan, over medium heat, heat remaining steak sauce mixture, water, margarine and cookie crumbs to a boil. Reduce heat and simmer 2 to 3 minutes or until thickened; keep warm.

Remove steak from marinade. Grill over medium heat for 15 to 20 minutes or until done, turning once. Slice steak and serve with warm sauce.
*Makes 6 servings*

# SAVORY GRILLED TOURNEDOS

⅓ cup A.1. Steak Sauce
¼ cup ketchup
¼ cup orange marmalade
2 tablespoons lemon juice
2 tablespoons minced onion
1 clove garlic, crushed
8 slices bacon (about 5 ounces)
8 (4-ounce) beef tenderloin steaks (tournedos),
    about 1 inch thick
Mushroom halves, radishes and parsley sprigs for garnish

In small bowl, blend steak sauce, ketchup, marmalade, lemon juice, onion and garlic; set aside.

Wrap a bacon slice around edge of each steak; secure with string or wooden toothpick. Grill steaks over medium-high heat for 10 minutes or until done, turning occasionally and brushing often with ½ cup prepared sauce. Remove toothpicks; serve steaks with remaining sauce. Garnish with mushroom halves, radishes and parsley if desired.

*Makes 8 servings*

# GRILLED STEAK WITH BLUE CHEESE SAUCE

½ cup heavy cream
½ cup A.1. Steak Sauce
¾ cup crumbled blue cheese (3 ounces)
1 tablespoon all-purpose flour
1 (1- to 1¼-pound) beef top round steak, about 1 inch thick
¼ cup sliced green onions

In small saucepan, over medium heat, heat heavy cream, ⅓ cup steak sauce, ½ cup cheese and flour, stirring constantly until cheese melts and mixture begins to boil; keep warm.

Grill steak over medium heat for 7 minutes on each side or until done, brushing occasionally with remaining steak sauce. Slice steak; serve topped with cheese sauce, remaining blue cheese and onions.

*Makes 4 servings*

# LEMON-PARSLEY SALMON STEAKS

½ cup A.1. Steak Sauce
½ cup parsley sprigs, finely chopped
¼ cup lemon juice
¼ cup finely chopped green onions
2 teaspoons sugar
2 cloves garlic, minced
½ teaspoon ground black pepper
4 (6- to 8-ounce) salmon steaks, about 1 inch thick

In small bowl, combine steak sauce, parsley, lemon juice, onions, sugar, garlic and pepper. Place salmon steaks in glass dish; coat with ½ cup parsley mixture. Cover; chill 1 hour, turning occasionally.

Remove steaks from marinade. Grill for 4 to 6 minutes on each side or until fish flakes easily when tested with fork, brushing often with reserved parsley mixture.

*Makes 4 servings*

# GRILLED STEAK AU POIVRE

½ cup A.1. Steak Sauce
1 (1½-pound) beef sirloin steak, ¾ inch thick
2 teaspoons cracked black pepper
½ cup dairy sour cream
2 tablespoons ketchup

Using 2 tablespoons steak sauce, brush both sides of steak; sprinkle 1 teaspoon pepper on each side, pressing into steak. Set aside.

In medium saucepan, over medium heat, combine remaining steak sauce, sour cream and ketchup. Cook and stir over low heat until heated through (do not boil); keep warm.

Grill steak over medium heat for 5 minutes on each side or until done. Serve steak with warm sauce.

*Makes 6 servings*

# STEAK RANCHERO

**⅔ cup A.1. Steak Sauce**
**⅔ cup mild, medium or hot thick and chunky salsa**
**2 tablespoons lime juice**
**1 (1-pound) beef top round steak, about ¾ inch thick**
**⅓ cup sliced ripe olives**
**4 cups shredded lettuce**
**⅓ cup dairy sour cream**

In small bowl, combine steak sauce, salsa and lime juice. Place steak in glass dish; coat both sides with ½ cup salsa mixture. Cover; chill 1 hour, turning occasionally.

In small saucepan, over medium heat, heat remaining salsa mixture. Reserve 2 tablespoons olives for garnish; stir remaining olives into sauce. Keep warm.

Remove steak from marinade. Grill over medium heat for 6 minutes on each side or until done, turning once.

To serve, arrange lettuce on serving platter. Thinly slice steak across grain; arrange over lettuce. Top with warm sauce and sour cream. Garnish with reserved olive slices.                                                      *Makes 4 servings*

# TENDERLOINS WITH ROASTED GARLIC SAUCE

**2 whole garlic bulbs, separated but not peeled (about 5 ounces)**
**⅔ cup A.1. Steak Sauce**
**¼ cup dry red wine**
**¼ cup finely chopped onion**
**4 (4- to 6-ounce) beef tenderloin steaks, about 1 inch thick**

Place unpeeled garlic cloves on baking sheet. Bake at 500°F for 15 to 20 minutes or until garlic is soft; cool. Squeeze garlic pulp from skins; chop pulp slightly. In small saucepan, combine garlic pulp, ½ cup steak sauce, wine and onion. Heat to a boil; reduce heat and simmer for 5 minutes. Keep warm.

Grill steaks over medium heat for 5 minutes on each side or until done, brushing occasionally with remaining steak sauce. Serve steak with warm garlic sauce.                                                      *Makes 4 servings*

## MUSHROOM-SAUCED STEAK

½ cup sliced onion
2 tablespoons margarine
1½ cups sliced mushrooms
1 cup A.1. BOLD Steak Sauce
½ cup dairy sour cream
2 (8-ounce) beef club or strip steaks, about 1 inch thick

In medium skillet, over medium heat, sauté onion in margarine until tender, about 5 minutes. Add mushrooms; sauté 5 minutes more. Stir in steak sauce; heat to a boil. Reduce heat and simmer 5 minutes; stir in sour cream. Cook and stir until heated through (do not boil); keep warm.

Grill steaks over medium heat for 5 minutes on each side or until done. Serve steaks topped with mushroom sauce.          *Makes 4 servings*

## GRILLED HERBED TURKEY TENDERLOINS

½ cup A.1. Steak Sauce
2 tablespoons dry sherry
2 tablespoons honey
2 tablespoons olive oil
1 tablespoon lemon juice
1 teaspoon rosemary leaves, crushed
½ teaspoon ground sage
2 pounds turkey tenderloins

In small bowl, combine steak sauce, sherry, honey, oil, lemon juice, rosemary and sage; reserve ½ cup sauce mixture. Place turkey tenderloins in glass dish; coat with remaining sauce. Cover; chill 1 hour, turning occasionally.

Remove turkey from marinade. Grill turkey over medium heat for 25 to 35 minutes or until done, turning occasionally. Meanwhile, in small saucepan, over medium heat, heat reserved sauce. Slice turkey; serve with warm sauce.          *Makes 6 to 8 servings*

# Beyond Beef

## HEALTHY GRILLED CHICKEN SALAD

½ cup A.1. Steak Sauce
½ cup prepared Italian salad dressing
1 teaspoon dried basil leaves
1 pound boneless chicken breast halves
6 cups mixed salad greens
¼ pound snow peas, blanched and halved
1 cup sliced mushrooms
1 medium red bell pepper, thinly sliced
Grated Parmesan cheese, optional

In small bowl, combine steak sauce, dressing and basil. Place chicken in glass dish; coat with ¼ cup marinade. Cover; chill 1 hour, turning occasionally.

Arrange salad greens, snow peas, mushrooms and pepper slices on 6 individual salad plates; set aside.

In small saucepan, over medium heat, heat remaining marinade mixture; keep warm.

Remove chicken from marinade. Grill over medium heat for 8 to 10 minutes or until done, turning occasionally. Thinly slice chicken; arrange over salad greens and drizzle warm dressing over prepared salad. Serve immediately, sprinkled with Parmesan cheese if desired. *Makes 6 servings*

Healthy Grilled Chicken Salad

## INDONESIAN PORK CHOPS 'N' ZESTY RELISH

¼ **cup A.1. Steak Sauce**
¼ **cup coconut milk**
 2 **tablespoons firmly packed light brown sugar**
 2 **cloves garlic, minced**
 1 **teaspoon grated fresh ginger**
½ **cup finely diced, seeded, peeled cucumber**
¼ **cup finely chopped radishes**
¼ **cup finely chopped onion**
¼ **cup shredded coconut, toasted**
 6 **(4-ounce) boneless loin pork chops**

In small bowl, combine steak sauce, coconut milk, brown sugar, garlic and ginger; reserve ¼ cup for basting. Stir cucumber, radishes, onion and coconut into remaining sauce; chill.

Grill pork chops over medium heat for 10 minutes or until done, turning occasionally and brushing often with reserved sauce. Serve hot with cucumber relish.                    *Makes 6 servings*

## SAVORY ONION GLAZED FOCACCIA

½ **cup finely chopped onion**
 3 **cloves garlic, minced**
¼ **cup olive oil**
 3 **tablespoons A.1. Steak Sauce**
 1 **(10-ounce) can refrigerated pizza crust dough**
 3 **tablespoons finely chopped parsley**
 3 **tablespoons finely chopped sundried tomato**
 1 **teaspoon dried oregano leaves**
½ **teaspoon coarsely ground black pepper**

In small skillet, over medium heat, sauté onion and garlic in 2 tablespoons oil until tender; remove from heat. Stir in steak sauce; set aside.

Unroll dough and flatten slightly; brush one side of dough with 1 tablespoon oil. Grill dough, oil side down, over low heat for 3 to 4 minutes or until dough is firm and brown. Brush top of dough with remaining oil and turn over on grill surface. Top evenly with steak sauce mixture, parsley, tomato, oregano and pepper. Grill 4 to 5 minutes or until bottom is golden; serve hot.                    *Makes 6 servings*

## SOUTH-OF-THE-BORDER VEGETABLE KABOBS

 5 cloves garlic, peeled
½ cup A.1. BOLD Steak Sauce
¼ cup margarine, melted
 1 tablespoon finely chopped cilantro
¾ teaspoon ground cumin
¼ teaspoon coarsely ground black pepper
⅛ teaspoon ground red pepper
 3 ears corn, cut crosswise into 1½-inch-thick slices and blanched
 3 medium plum tomatoes, cut into ½-inch slices
 1 small zucchini, cut lengthwise into thin slices
 1 cup baby carrots, blanched

Mince 1 garlic clove; halve remaining garlic cloves and set aside. In small bowl, combine steak sauce, margarine, cilantro, minced garlic, cumin and peppers; set aside.

Alternately thread vegetables and halved garlic cloves onto 6 (10-inch) metal skewers. Grill kabobs over medium heat for 7 to 9 minutes or until done, turning and basting often with steak sauce mixture. Remove from skewers; serve immediately.                           *Makes 6 servings*

# BARBECUED LEG OF LAMB

⅓ cup A.1. Steak Sauce
 2 tablespoons red wine vinegar
 2 tablespoons vegetable oil
 1 teaspoon chili powder
 1 teaspoon dried oregano leaves
½ teaspoon coarsely ground black pepper
½ teaspoon ground cinnamon
 2 cloves garlic, crushed
 1 (5- to 6-pound) leg of lamb, boned, butterflied and trimmed of
     fat (about 3 pounds after boning)

In small bowl, combine steak sauce, vinegar, oil, chili powder, oregano, pepper, cinnamon and garlic. Place lamb in nonmetal dish; coat with steak sauce mixture. Cover; chill 1 hour, turning occasionally.

Remove lamb from marinade. Grill over medium heat for 25 to 35 minutes or until done, turning often. Cut lamb into thin slices; serve hot.
                                          *Makes 12 servings*

# HOT 'N' SPICY CHICKEN BARBECUE

**½ cup A.1. Steak Sauce**
**½ cup tomato sauce**
**¼ cup finely chopped onion**
**2 tablespoons cider vinegar**
**2 tablespoons maple syrup**
**1 tablespoon vegetable oil**
**2 teaspoons chili powder**
**½ teaspoon crushed red pepper flakes**
**1 (3-pound) chicken, cut up**

In medium saucepan, combine steak sauce, tomato sauce, onion, vinegar, maple syrup, oil, chili powder and red pepper flakes. Over medium heat, heat mixture to a boil; reduce heat. Simmer for 5 to 7 minutes or until thickened; cool.

Grill chicken over medium heat for 30 to 40 minutes or until done, turning and basting frequently with prepared sauce. Serve hot.

*Makes 4 servings*

# FISH IN FOIL

**1 (8-ounce) can stewed tomatoes**
**⅓ cup A.1. BOLD Steak Sauce**
**1 clove garlic, minced**
**4 (4-ounce) firm fish fillets**
**2 cups frozen mixed vegetables**

In small bowl, combine stewed tomatoes, steak sauce and garlic; set aside.

Place each fish fillet in center of heavy duty or double thickness foil; top each with ½ cup mixed vegetables and ¼ cup steak sauce mixture. Wrap foil securely.

Grill fish packets over medium heat for 8 to 10 minutes or until fish flakes easily with fork. Serve immediately.

*Makes 4 servings*

# TANGY PINEAPPLE FONDUE

1 (8-ounce) can crushed pineapple in its own juice, undrained
1 cup apple juice
¼ cup A.1. Steak Sauce
¼ cup firmly packed light brown sugar
1 tablespoon cornstarch
1 medium pineapple, cut into chunks
1 (12-ounce) package prepared pound cake, cut into 1-inch
  cubes
1 pint strawberries, halved
1 large Granny Smith apple, cored and cut into chunks

In small saucepan, combine crushed pineapple, apple juice, steak sauce, brown sugar and cornstarch until blended. Over medium heat, cook and stir pineapple mixture until boiling; reduce heat. Simmer 1 minute; keep warm.

Alternately thread pineapple chunks and cake cubes onto 16 (10-inch) metal skewers. Over medium heat, grill kabobs until lightly toasted, about 3 to 5 minutes, turning occasionally. Remove pineapple chunks and cake cubes from skewers; arrange on large platter with remaining fruit. Serve with warm sauce for dipping.                          *Makes 16 servings*

# TANDOORI-STYLE CHICKEN

½ cup plain regular or lowfat yogurt
¼ cup A.1. Steak Sauce
¼ cup chopped fresh mint
1 teaspoon paprika
½ teaspoon ground red pepper
3 cloves garlic, crushed
1 (2½- to 3-pound) chicken, cut into 4 pieces
  Raita (recipe follows)

In small bowl, combine yogurt, steak sauce, mint, paprika, red pepper and garlic. Place chicken pieces in glass dish; coat with yogurt mixture. Cover; chill 1 hour, turning occasionally.

Remove chicken from marinade. Grill chicken over medium heat for 30 to 35 minutes or until done, turning occasionally. Serve with Raita.
                                                    *Makes 4 servings*

**Raita:** In small bowl, combine ½ cup plain regular or lowfat yogurt; ½ cup finely diced, seeded, peeled cucumber; 1 tablespoon A.1. Steak Sauce; 1 tablespoon finely chopped fresh mint and 2 teaspoons honey. Cover; chill until serving time.

# Burger Basics

## BIG D RANCH BURGERS

1 cup sliced onions
⅓ cup sliced green bell pepper strips
⅓ cup sliced red bell pepper strips
1 tablespoon margarine
3 tablespoons A.1. Steak Sauce
2 teaspoons prepared horseradish
1 pound ground beef
4 onion rolls, split

In medium skillet, over medium heat, cook onions, green pepper and red pepper in margarine until tender-crisp. Stir in steak sauce and horseradish; keep warm.

Shape ground beef into 4 patties. Grill burgers over medium heat for 5 minutes on each side or until done. Place burgers on roll bottoms; top each with ¼ cup pepper mixture and roll top. Serve immediately.

*Makes 4 servings*

## VEGETARIAN BURGERS

½ cup A.1. Steak Sauce
¼ cup plain yogurt
⅔ cup slivered almonds
⅔ cup salted peanuts
⅔ cup sunflower kernels
½ cup chopped green bell pepper
¼ cup chopped onion
1 clove garlic, minced
1 tablespoon red wine vinegar
4 (5-inch) pita breads, halved
4 lettuce leaves
4 tomato slices

In small bowl, combine ¼ cup steak sauce and yogurt; set aside.

In food processor or blender, process almonds, peanuts, sunflower kernels, green pepper, onion and garlic until coarsely chopped. With motor running, slowly add remaining steak sauce and vinegar until blended; shape mixture into 4 patties.

Grill burgers over medium heat for 1½ minutes on each side or until heated through, turning once. Split open top edge of each pita bread. Layer lettuce, burger, tomato slice and 2 tablespoons prepared sauce in each pita bread half. Serve immediately.                      *Makes 4 servings*

**Note:** Sauce may also be served with beef burgers.

## BLACK GOLD BURGER

¾ cup finely chopped onion
6 large cloves garlic, minced (about 3 tablespoons)
2 tablespoons margarine
1 tablespoon sugar
¾ cup A.1. BOLD Steak Sauce
1½ pounds ground beef
6 hamburger rolls, split

In medium skillet, over medium heat, cook and stir onion and garlic in margarine until tender but not brown; stir in sugar. Reduce heat to low; cook for 10 minutes. Stir in steak sauce; keep warm.

Shape ground beef into 6 patties. Grill burgers over medium heat for 5 minutes on each side or until done. Place burgers on roll bottoms; top each with 3 tablespoons sauce and roll top. Serve immediately; garnish as desired.                                           *Makes 6 servings*

**Note:** Sauce may also be served with steaks or roast beef.

Vegetarian Burger

## AMERICA'S FAVORITE CHEDDAR BEEF BURGERS

- **1 pound ground beef**
- **⅓ cup A.1. Steak Sauce**
- **1 medium onion, cut into strips**
- **1 medium green or red bell pepper, cut into strips**
- **1 tablespoon margarine**
- **4 ounces Cheddar cheese, sliced**
- **4 hamburger rolls**
- **4 tomato slices**

In medium bowl, combine ground beef and 3 tablespoons steak sauce; shape mixture into 4 patties. Set aside.

In medium skillet, over medium heat, cook onion and pepper in margarine until tender, stirring occasionally. Stir in remaining steak sauce; keep warm.

Grill burgers over medium heat for 4 minutes on each side or until done. When almost done, top with cheese; grill until cheese melts. Spoon 2 tablespoons onion mixture onto each roll bottom; top each with burger, tomato slice, some of remaining onion mixture and roll top. Serve immediately.        *Makes 4 servings*

## BURGERS CANADIAN

- **½ cup mayonnaise**
- **⅓ cup A.1. Steak Sauce**
- **2 tablespoons prepared horseradish**
- **1 pound ground beef**
- **2 ounces Cheddar cheese, sliced**
- **4 slices Canadian bacon (4 ounces)**
- **4 sesame sandwich rolls, split and lightly toasted**
- **4 curly lettuce leaves**

In small bowl, combine mayonnaise, steak sauce and horseradish. Cover; chill until serving time.

Shape ground beef into 4 patties. Grill burgers over medium heat for 4 minutes on each side. When almost done, top with cheese; grill until cheese melts. Grill Canadian bacon over medium heat for 1 minute on each side or until heated through. Spread 2 tablespoons sauce on each roll bottom; top with burger, warm Canadian bacon slice, lettuce leaf and roll top. Serve immediately with remaining sauce for dipping.        *Makes 4 servings*

## SAVORY STUFFED TURKEY BURGERS

**1 pound ground turkey**
**¼ cup A.1. BOLD Steak Sauce**
**¼ cup chopped onion**
**½ teaspoon dried thyme leaves**
**¼ teaspoon ground black pepper**
**½ cup prepared herb bread stuffing**
**½ cup whole berry cranberry sauce**
**4 slices whole wheat bread, toasted**
**4 lettuce leaves**

In medium bowl, combine turkey, 2 tablespoons steak sauce, onion, thyme and pepper; shape into 8 thin patties. Place 2 tablespoons prepared stuffing in center of each of 4 patties. Top with remaining patties. Seal edges to form 4 patties; set aside.

In small bowl; combine remaining 2 tablespoons steak sauce and cranberry sauce; set aside.

Grill burgers over medium heat for 10 minutes on each side or until done. Top each bread slice with lettuce leaf and burger. Serve immediately topped with prepared cranberry sauce mixture.          *Makes 4 servings*

## BACON BLUE BURGERS

**1 pound ground beef**
**½ cup A.1. Steak Sauce**
**½ cup crumbled blue cheese (2 ounces)**
**4 sandwich rolls, split**
**4 curly lettuce leaves**
**4 thin red onion slices**
**4 bacon slices, cooked and halved (about 3 ounces)**

In medium bowl, combine ground beef and 3 tablespoons steak sauce; shape mixture into 4 patties. Set aside.

In small bowl, stir together remaining steak sauce and blue cheese; set aside.

Grill burgers over medium heat for 5 minutes on each side or until done. Spread 1 tablespoon steak sauce mixture onto each roll bottom; top each with lettuce leaf, onion slice, burger and 2 bacon halves. Spread 1 tablespoon steak sauce mixture on each roll top; close rolls. Serve immediately.          *Makes 4 servings*

# BURRITO BURGERS

**6 tablespoons A.1. Steak Sauce**
**1 (4-ounce) can diced green chiles**
**3 tablespoons dairy sour cream**
**1 pound ground beef**
**4 (6½-inch) flour tortillas**
**1 cup shredded lettuce**
**½ cup shredded Cheddar cheese (2 ounces)**
**Shredded Cheddar cheese, for garnish**

In small bowl, combine 2 tablespoons steak sauce, 2 tablespoons chiles and sour cream. Cover; chill until serving time.

In medium bowl, combine ground beef, remaining steak sauce and chiles. Shape mixture into 4 (4-inch) oval patties. Grill over medium heat for 5 minutes on each side or until done. Place lettuce in center of each tortilla; top each with burger, prepared sauce and cheese. Fold edges of tortilla in like a burrito; garnish with additional shredded cheese. Serve immediately.

*Makes 4 servings*

# MEDITERRANEAN BURGERS

**½ cup feta cheese (2 ounces)**
**¼ cup A.1. Steak Sauce**
**2 tablespoons sliced ripe olives**
**2 tablespoons mayonnaise**
**1 pound ground beef**
**4 regular pita breads**
**4 lettuce leaves**
**4 tomato slices**

In small bowl, combine feta cheese, 2 tablespoons steak sauce, olives and mayonnaise. Cover; chill until ready to serve.

Shape beef into 4 patties; grill over medium heat for 5 minutes on each side or until done, brushing with remaining 2 tablespoons steak sauce. Split open top edge of each pita bread. Place 1 lettuce leaf in each pita pocket; top each with burger, tomato slice and 2 tablespoons prepared sauce. Serve immediately.

*Makes 4 servings*

# BLACKENED BURGERS

**1 pound ground beef**
**5 tablespoons A.1. Steak Sauce**
**4 teaspoons coarsely cracked black pepper**
**4 kaiser rolls, split**
**4 tomato slices**

In medium bowl, combine ground beef, 3 tablespoons steak sauce and 1 teaspoon pepper; shape mixture into 4 patties. Brush patties with remaining steak sauce; coat with remaining pepper.

Grill burgers over medium heat for 5 minutes on each side or until done. Top each roll bottom with burger, tomato slice and roll top. Serve immediately. *Makes 4 servings*

# SUPER CHEESEBURGER

**1 pound ground beef**
**½ cup chopped onion**
**¼ cup chopped green bell pepper**
**1 tablespoon margarine**
**2 teaspoons all-purpose flour**
**⅓ cup milk**
**⅓ cup diced processed American cheese (1½ ounces)**
**⅓ cup A.1. Steak Sauce**
**1 cup shredded lettuce**

In medium bowl, combine ground beef and onion; shape mixture into 1 (7-inch) patty. Set aside.

In medium skillet, over medium heat, cook and stir green pepper in margarine until tender-crisp; blend in flour. Gradually stir in milk; cook and stir until mixture thickens and begins to boil. Reduce heat to low; add cheese, stirring until melted. Stir in steak sauce until blended. Keep warm.

Grill burger over medium heat for 7 minutes on each side or until done. Arrange lettuce on serving plate; top with grilled burger and cheese sauce. Cut into wedges to serve. *Makes 4 servings*

# Grill Crazy

## BEEF AND BACON SHISH KABOBS

½ cup A.1. Steak Sauce
¼ cup sherry cooking wine
2 tablespoons honey
1 (1-pound) beef sirloin steak, cut into 1-inch cubes
14 slices bacon, halved crosswise (about ½ pound)
1 large onion, cut into wedges
1 large green or red bell pepper, cut into squares
12 small mushroom caps

In small bowl, blend steak sauce, sherry and honey. Place beef cubes in nonmetal dish; coat with ¼ cup steak sauce mixture. Cover; chill 1 hour, stirring occasionally.

Remove beef cubes from marinade. Wrap half bacon slice around each cube. Alternately thread beef and bacon cubes, onion, pepper and mushrooms onto 4 (10-inch) metal skewers. Grill over medium heat for 8 to 10 minutes or until done, turning and brushing occasionally with reserved steak sauce mixture. Serve immediately. *Makes 4 servings*

Beef and Bacon Shish Kabob

# GRILLED BEEF 'N' VEGETABLE-TOPPED PIZZA

1 pound ground beef
¾ cup prepared spaghetti sauce
½ cup A.1. BOLD Steak Sauce
1 pound frozen bread or pizza dough, thawed
2 tablespoons olive oil
2 cups shredded mozzarella cheese (8 ounces)
¼ cup chopped tomato
¼ cup sliced green onions
¼ cup sliced ripe olives

In medium skillet, over medium-high heat, brown ground beef until no longer pink, stirring to break up beef; drain. Stir in spaghetti sauce and steak sauce; cook and stir until heated through. Keep warm.

Divide dough in half; shape each piece into 8-inch round. Brush one side of each dough round with oil. Grill pizza dough rounds, oil side down, over low heat for 5 to 7 minutes or until dough is firm and brown. Brush tops of dough rounds with oil and turn over on grill surface. Top each with half the beef mixture, cheese, tomato, onions and olives. Grill, covered with lid or foil, for 5 to 7 minutes or until bottoms are golden and cheese melts. Serve immediately.                        *Makes 2 (8-inch) pizza rounds*

# TERIYAKI STEAK STRIPS

½ cup A.1. Steak Sauce
2 tablespoons soy sauce
2 tablespoons firmly packed light brown sugar
2 cloves garlic, minced
1 teaspoon ground ginger
1 (1-pound) boneless beef sirloin steak, about 1 inch thick, thinly sliced
2 cups fresh or canned pineapple chunks
2 bell peppers (red and/or green), cut into squares
    Hot cooked rice

In small bowl, combine steak sauce, soy sauce, brown sugar, garlic and ginger. Place steak slices in nonmetal bowl; coat with ¼ cup steak sauce mixture. Cover; chill 1 hour, stirring occasionally.

Remove steak from marinade. Alternately thread steak, pineapple and pepper onto 8 (12-inch) metal skewers. Grill over medium heat for 5 minutes or until done, turning and brushing occasionally with remaining steak sauce mixture. Serve immediately over rice if desired.
                        *Makes 8 servings*

# GRILLED STEAK AND ASPARAGUS SALAD

½ **cup bottled light olive oil vinaigrette**
⅓ **cup A.1. Steak Sauce**
1 **(1-pound) beef top round steak**
1 **(10-ounce) package frozen asparagus spears, cooked and**
   **cooled**
½ **cup thinly sliced red bell pepper**
8 **large lettuce leaves**
1 **tablespoon toasted sesame seed**

In small bowl, blend vinaigrette and steak sauce. Place steak in glass dish; coat with ¼ cup vinaigrette mixture. Cover; chill 1 hour, turning once.

In small saucepan, over medium heat, heat remaining vinaigrette mixture to a boil. Reduce heat and simmer 1 minute; keep warm.

Remove steak from marinade. Grill over medium heat for 12 minutes or until done, turning occasionally. Thinly slice steak. Arrange steak, asparagus and red pepper on lettuce leaves. Pour warm marinade over salad; sprinkle with sesame seed. Serve immediately.

*Makes 4 servings*


# 3-STAR HOT PEPPER ROULADES

1 **(1-pound) beef top round steak, about ½ inch thick**
⅓ **cup A.1. Steak Sauce**
½ **teaspoon coarsely ground black pepper**
¼ **teaspoon ground red pepper**
¼ **teaspoon ground white pepper**

Pound steak to ¼-inch thickness. Spread 2 tablespoons steak sauce over steak. Sprinkle peppers evenly over steak sauce. Roll up steak from short edge. To make roulades, cut steak crosswise into 8 rolled slices. Thread 2 roulades securely onto each of 4 (10-inch) metal skewers.

Grill roulades over medium heat for 8 to 10 minutes or until done, turning and brushing occasionally with remaining steak sauce. Serve immediately.

*Makes 4 servings*

# BEEF SATÉ STRIPS

¾ **cup A.1. Steak Sauce**
⅓ **cup chunky peanut butter**
2 **tablespoons teriyaki sauce**
1 **(1-pound) beef flank steak, thinly sliced**
1 **cup (1-inch) green onion pieces (about 1 bunch)**
½ **cup beef broth**
1 **teaspoon cornstarch**
5 **lime wedges, for garnish**
  **Hot cooked rice**

In small bowl, combine steak sauce, peanut butter and teriyaki sauce. Place steak strips in glass dish; coat with ⅔ cup prepared steak sauce mixture. Cover; chill 1 hour, stirring occasionally.

Soak 5 (12-inch) wooden skewers in water for at least 30 minutes. Remove steak strips from marinade. Alternately thread steak strips and onion pieces onto skewers. Grill over medium heat for 6 to 8 minutes or until done, turning occasionally. Meanwhile, in small saucepan, over medium heat, cook and stir remaining steak sauce mixture, beef broth and cornstarch until mixture thickens and begins to boil. Garnish steak with lime wedges. Serve over rice with prepared sauce.        *Makes 5 servings*

# PESTO BEEF SWIRLS

⅓ **cup A.1. Steak Sauce**
¼ **cup grated Parmesan cheese**
¼ **cup pignoli nuts or walnuts**
2 **tablespoons dried basil leaves**
2 **cloves garlic**
1 **(2-pound) beef flank steak, pounded to ½-inch thickness**

In blender or food processor, blend all ingredients except steak to a coarse paste; spread over top of steak. Cut steak across grain into eight 1-inch-wide strips. Roll up each strip from short edge; secure with wooden toothpick.

Grill over medium heat for 7 to 8 minutes on each side or until done, brushing often with additional steak sauce. Remove toothpicks; serve immediately.        *Makes 8 servings*

# FAJITA KABOBS

½ cup A.1. Steak Sauce
½ cup mild, medium or hot thick and chunky salsa
1 (1½-pound) beef top round steak, cut into thin strips
2 large red onions, cut into wedges
2 large green bell peppers, cut into ¾-inch-wide strips
12 (6½-inch) flour tortillas, warmed
   Dairy sour cream

In small bowl, blend steak sauce and salsa. Place steak strips in nonmetal bowl; coat with ½ cup salsa mixture. Cover; chill 1 hour, stirring occasionally.

Remove steak from marinade. Alternately thread steak, onions and peppers onto 6 (10-inch) metal skewers. Grill kabobs over medium heat for 10 to 15 minutes or until done, turning occasionally and brushing with remaining salsa mixture. Serve immediately with tortillas, sour cream and additional steak sauce.                              *Makes 6 servings*

# GRILLED STEAK AND PEPPER SANDWICHES

1 (1-pound) beef top round steak
¾ cup A.1. Steak Sauce
2 bell peppers (1 red and 1 green), sliced
4 large hard rolls, split and grilled
4 ounces thinly sliced mozzarella cheese

Place steak in nonmetal dish; coat with ¼ cup steak sauce. Cover; chill 1 hour, turning occasionally.

In medium skillet, over medium heat, cook and stir peppers in remaining steak sauce until tender-crisp, about 10 minutes; keep warm.

Remove steak from marinade. Grill over medium heat for 6 minutes on each side or until done. Thinly slice steak; arrange on roll bottoms. Top each with warm pepper sauce, cheese slice and roll top; serve immediately.                                       *Makes 4 servings*

## CURRIED BEEF PITAS

¾ **cup A.1. Steak Sauce**
  1 **(8-ounce) can pineapple chunks in unsweetened juice,**
     **drained (reserve juice)**
1½ **teaspoons curry powder**
  1 **(1-pound) beef top round steak, thinly sliced**
  1 **large green bell pepper, cut into squares**
  2 **medium onions, cut into wedges**
½ **cup lowfat lemon yogurt**
  6 **(5-inch) pita breads, halved**

Soak 6 (12-inch) wooden skewers in water for at least 30 minutes. In small bowl, combine steak sauce, ¼ cup reserved pineapple juice and curry powder; set aside.

Alternately thread beef strips, pepper, onions and pineapple chunks onto skewers. Place skewers in glass dish; coat with ½ cup steak sauce mixture. Cover; chill 1 hour, turning occasionally.

In small saucepan, over medium heat, heat remaining steak sauce mixture to a boil. Cool slightly and slowly stir in yogurt; keep warm. (Do not boil.)

Remove skewers from marinade. Grill over medium heat for 10 to 15 minutes or until done, turning occasionally. Split open top edge of each pita bread half. Remove beef strips, vegetables and pineapple from skewers; arrange in pita pockets. Serve hot with warm sauce. *Makes 6 servings*

## FRUIT GLAZED BEEF RIBS

  4 **pounds beef back ribs, cut into individual ribs**
⅓ **cup A.1. BOLD Steak Sauce**
¼ **cup ketchup**
¼ **cup apricot preserves**
  1 **tablespoon lemon juice**
½ **teaspoon grated lemon peel**

Arrange ribs on rack in large roasting pan. Bake at 400°F for 30 minutes.

In small saucepan, over medium heat, cook and stir steak sauce, ketchup, preserves, lemon juice and lemon peel until blended. Grill ribs over medium heat for 20 minutes or until done, turning and brushing often with prepared sauce. Serve hot. *Makes 6 to 8 servings*

# GRILLED MEAT LOAF
# AND POTATOES

**1 pound ground beef**
**½ cup A.1. Steak Sauce**
**½ cup plain dry bread crumbs**
**1 egg**
**¼ cup finely chopped green bell pepper**
**¼ cup finely chopped onion**
**2 tablespoons margarine, melted**
**4 (6-ounce) red skin potatoes, parboiled and sliced into**
     **¼-inch-thick rounds**
**Grated Parmesan cheese**

In large bowl, combine ground beef, ¼ cup steak sauce, bread crumbs, egg, pepper and onion. Divide mixture and shape into 4 (4-inch) oval loaves.

In small bowl, combine remaining steak sauce and margarine; set aside.

Over medium heat, grill meat loaves for 20 to 25 minutes and potato slices for 10 to 12 minutes, turning and brushing both occasionally with steak sauce mixture. Sprinkle potatoes with Parmesan cheese; serve immediately.                                            *Makes 4 servings*


# WILTED STEAK SALAD

**½ cup A.1. Steak Sauce**
**⅓ cup red wine vinegar**
**¼ cup vegetable oil**
**1 (1-pound) beef top round steak**
**6 cups torn mixed salad greens**
**1 cup cherry tomato halves**
**½ cup sliced cucumber**
**¼ cup crumbled blue cheese, optional**

In small bowl, blend steak sauce, vinegar and oil. Place steak in glass dish; coat with ¼ cup steak sauce mixture. Cover; chill 1 hour, turning occasionally.

In small saucepan, over medium heat, heat remaining steak sauce mixture to a boil; reduce heat and simmer 1 minute. Keep warm.

Remove steak from marinade. Grill over medium heat for 6 minutes on each side or until done. Cut steak into thin slices. In salad bowl, arrange salad greens, steak, tomatoes and cucumber. Pour warm marinade over salad; top with blue cheese if desired. Toss to coat well; serve immediately.
                                                       *Makes 6 servings*

# Rainy Day Favorites

## SKILLET STEAK FAJITAS

½ cup A.1. Steak Sauce
½ cup mild, medium or hot thick and chunky salsa
1 (1-pound) beef flank or bottom round steak, thinly sliced
1 medium onion, thinly sliced
1 medium green bell pepper, cut into strips
1 tablespoon margarine
8 (6½-inch) flour tortillas, warmed

Blend steak sauce and salsa. Place steak in glass dish; coat with ¼ cup salsa mixture. Cover; chill 1 hour, stirring occasionally.

In large skillet, over medium-high heat, cook onion and pepper in margarine for 3 minutes or until tender. Remove with slotted spoon; set aside. In same skillet, cook and stir steak for 5 minutes or until done. Add remaining salsa mixture, onion and pepper; cook until heated through. Serve with tortillas and your favorite fajita toppings if desired.

*Makes 4 servings*

## CHICKEN STIR-FRY

½ cup A.1. Steak Sauce
¼ cup dry white wine
2 tablespoons Dijon mustard
2 tablespoons soy sauce
1 tablespoon sesame oil
2 cloves garlic, crushed
½ teaspoon ground black pepper
1½ pounds boneless chicken breasts, cut into ½-inch strips
1 cup sliced carrots
1 cup thinly sliced red bell pepper
1 cup snow peas
1 cup sliced onion
    Hot cooked rice, optional

In medium nonmetal bowl, whisk together steak sauce, wine, mustard, soy sauce, sesame oil, garlic and black pepper; add chicken, stirring to coat. Cover; chill 1 hour, stirring occasionally.

In large skillet, over medium-high heat, cook and stir chicken mixture until no longer pink, about 5 minutes. Add vegetables; cook and stir until tender, about 5 to 7 minutes. Serve over rice if desired.          *Makes 6 servings*

## BOLD BEEF STROGANOFF

1 cup thinly sliced onion
3 tablespoons margarine
3 cups thinly sliced mushrooms
1 (1½-pound) beef flank steak, thinly sliced across the grain
¾ cup A.1. BOLD Steak Sauce
½ cup dairy sour cream
    Hot cooked noodles

In large skillet, over medium-high heat, cook onion in 1 tablespoon margarine for 2 to 3 minutes. Add mushrooms; cook just until tender. Remove from skillet.

In same skillet, brown meat in batches in remaining margarine. Return meat and vegetables to skillet. Stir in steak sauce. Heat to boil; reduce heat to low. Simmer for 15 minutes. Stir in sour cream. Serve immediately over noodles.          *Makes 6 servings*

# 30-MINUTE CHILI OLÉ

**1 cup chopped onion**
**2 cloves garlic, minced**
**1 tablespoon vegetable oil**
**2 pounds ground beef**
**1 (15-ounce) can tomato sauce**
**1 (14½-ounce) can stewed tomatoes**
**¾ cup A.1. Steak Sauce**
**1 tablespoon chili powder**
**1 teaspoon ground cumin**
**1 (16-ounce) can black beans, rinsed and drained**
**1 (11-ounce) can corn, drained**
  **Shredded cheese, sour cream and chopped tomato, for**
    **garnish**

In 6-quart heavy pot, over medium-high heat, sauté onion and garlic in oil until tender. Add beef; cook and stir until brown. Drain; stir in tomato sauce, stewed tomatoes, steak sauce, chili powder and cumin. Heat to a boil; reduce heat to low. Cover; simmer for 10 minutes, stirring occasionally. Stir in beans and corn; simmer, uncovered, for 10 minutes. Serve hot, garnished with cheese, sour cream and tomato.

*Makes 8 servings*

# SPICY BARBECUE BEEF SANDWICH

**1 cup A.1. Steak Sauce**
**⅔ cup chili sauce**
**½ cup water**
**3 tablespoons Dijon mustard**
**1 (2-pound) beef top round steak**
**2 tablespoons vegetable oil**
**2 large onions, sliced**
**8 sandwich rolls, split and toasted**

In small bowl, combine steak sauce, chili sauce, water and mustard; set aside.

In large heavy saucepan, over medium-high heat, brown steak in oil. Add onions, stirring until lightly browned. Stir in sauce mixture; heat to a boil. Cover; reduce heat and simmer 1½ hours or until steak is tender. Remove steak; cut into julienne strips. Return steak to pan; cook and stir until hot. Spoon steak mixture onto roll bottoms; replace tops. Serve immediately.

*Makes 8 servings*

## PHILADELPHIA CHEESE STEAK SANDWICHES

**2 cups sliced red or green bell peppers (about 2 medium)**
**1 small onion, thinly sliced**
**1 tablespoon vegetable oil**
**½ cup A.1. BOLD Steak Sauce**
**1 teaspoon prepared horseradish**
**8 ounces thinly sliced beef sandwich steaks**
**4 long sandwich rolls, split**
**4 ounces thinly sliced mozzarella cheese**

In medium saucepan, over medium heat, sauté pepper and onion slices in oil until tender. Stir in steak sauce and horseradish; keep warm.

In lightly greased medium skillet, over medium-high heat, cook sandwich steaks until done. On roll bottoms, portion beef, pepper mixture and cheese.

Broil sandwich bottoms 4 inches from heat source for 3 to 5 minutes or until cheese melts; replace tops. Serve immediately.

*Makes 4 sandwiches*

## STIR-FRY BEEF 'N' BROCCOLI

**½ cup A.1. Steak Sauce**
**¼ cup soy sauce**
**2 cloves garlic, crushed**
**1 (1-pound) beef top round steak, thinly sliced**
**1 tablespoon vegetable oil**
**1 (16-ounce) bag frozen combination broccoli, red bell**
   **peppers, bamboo shoots and mushrooms, thawed***
**Hot cooked rice, optional**

In small bowl, blend steak sauce, soy sauce and garlic. Place steak in glass dish; coat with ¼ cup steak sauce mixture. Cover; chill 1 hour, stirring occasionally. Reserve remaining sauce mixture.

In large, lightly greased skillet, over medium-high heat, stir-fry steak in oil 3 to 4 minutes or until steak is no longer pink. Remove steak with slotted spoon; keep warm.

In same skillet, heat vegetables and reserved sauce mixture to a boil; reduce heat. Cover; simmer for 2 to 3 minutes. Stir in steak. Serve over rice if desired.

*Makes 4 servings*

*1 (16-ounce) package frozen broccoli cuts may be substituted.

Philadelphia Cheese Steak
Sandwich

## BEEF 'N' BRIE SANDWICHES

**8 slices rye bread**
**8 thin slices rare roast beef (8 ounces)**
**½ cup A.1. Steak Sauce**
**6 ounces Brie cheese, sliced**
**1 large tomato, thinly sliced**
**2 tablespoons margarine, softened**

On each of 4 bread slices, place 2 slices roast beef; spread each with 2 tablespoons steak sauce. Top with cheese, tomato slices and remaining bread slices. Spread margarine on both sides of sandwiches. Toast on both sides in lightly greased skillet; serve immediately.

*Makes 4 servings*

## STEAK DIANE

**¼ cup minced shallots**
**2 tablespoons margarine**
**2 boneless beef club or strip steaks, about ½ inch thick**
**½ cup A.1. BOLD Steak Sauce**
**1 tablespoon capers**
**1 clove garlic, minced**
**1 tablespoon minced parsley**

In large skillet, over medium heat, sauté shallots in 1 tablespoon margarine until tender, about 5 minutes. Increase heat to high; add remaining margarine to skillet. Add steaks; brown on both sides, about 2 minutes. Reduce heat to medium; stir in steak sauce, capers and garlic. Simmer 2 minutes; add parsley. Serve immediately. *Makes 2 servings*

# INDEX

A.1. Dry Spice Rub, 38
A.1. Grilled Fish Steaks, 38
A.1. Virgin Mary, 12
Almond Chicken Kabobs, 20
America's Favorite Cheddar Beef Burgers, 66
**Appetizers**
  A.1. Virgin Mary, 12
  Almond Chicken Kabobs, 20
  Asian Beef Bites, 16
  Barbecue Ribettes, 18
  Beefy Nachos, 20
  Cowboy Kabobs, 12
  Fiesta Chicken Wings, 12
  Greek Grilled Pizza Wedges, 18
  Grilled Antipasto, 10
  Grilled Fruit Kabobs, 22
  Hot Blue Cheese Dip with Grilled Vegetables, 14
  Sunshine Chicken Drumsticks, 14
  Surf and Turf Brochettes, 16
  Thai Chicken Ribbons, 22
Apricot-Glazed Ham Steaks, 42
Asian Beef Bites, 16

Bacon Blue Burgers, 68
Barbecue Ribettes, 18
Barbecued Leg of Lamb, 56
**Bastes** (*see also* **Marinades, Sauces**)
  Curried Barbecue Sauce, 32
  Honey Basting Sauce, 26
  Orange Barbecue Sauce, 28
  Quick Barbecue Basting Sauce, 26
  Tangy Lemon Glaze, 27
**Beef** (*see also* **Beef, Ground**)
  A.1. Dry Spice Rub, 38
  Asian Beef Bites, 16
  Beef and Bacon Shish Kabobs, 72
  Beef 'n' Brie Sandwiches, 92
  Beef Saté Strips, 78
  Bold Beef Stroganoff, 86
  Citrus Grilled Steak, 40
  Cowboy Kabobs, 12
  Curried Beef Pitas, 80
  Fajita Kabobs, 79
  Fruit Glazed Beef Ribs, 80
  Gazpacho Steak Roll, 36
  Greek Grilled Pizza Wedges, 18
  Grilled Antipasto, 10
  Grilled Sauerbraten Steak, 43
  Grilled Steak and Asparagus Salad, 76
  Grilled Steak and Pepper Sandwiches, 79
  Grilled Steak au Poivre, 46
  Grilled Steak with Blue Cheese Sauce, 44
  Hearty Grilled Tenderloins, 40
  Mexican Flank Steak, 34
  Mushroom-Sauced Steak, 50
  Pesto Beef Swirls, 78
  Philadelphia Cheese Steak Sandwiches, 90
  Savory Grilled Tournedos, 44
  Skillet Steak Fajitas, 84
  Spicy Barbecue Beef Sandwich, 88
  Steak Diane, 92
  Steak Ranchero, 48
  Steak with Horseradish Sauce, 43
  Stir-Fry Beef 'n' Broccoli, 90
  Surf and Turf Brochettes, 16

  Tenderloins with Roasted Garlic Sauce, 48
  Teriyaki Steak Strips, 74
  3-Star Hot Pepper Roulades, 76
  Tijuana Blackened Steak, 36
  Tournedos with Mushroom Wine Sauce, 42
  Wilted Steak Salad, 82
  Zesty Lemon-Glazed Steak, 34
**Beef, Ground**
  America's Favorite Cheddar Beef Burgers, 66
  Bacon Blue Burgers, 68
  Beefy Nachos, 20
  Big D Ranch Burgers, 62
  Blackened Burgers, 71
  Black Gold Burgers, 64
  Burgers Canadian, 66
  Burrito Burgers, 70
  Grilled Beef 'n' Vegetable-Topped Pizza, 74
  Grilled Meat Loaf and Potatoes, 82
  Mediterranean Burgers, 70
  Super Cheeseburger, 71
  30-Minute Chili Olé, 88
Beefy Nachos, 20
Big D Ranch Burgers, 62
Blackened Burgers, 71
Black Gold Burgers, 64
Bold Beef Stroganoff, 86
Bold Mushroom Sauce, 27
Bold Pepper Sauce, 30
Burgers Canadian, 66
Burrito Burgers, 70

**Chicken**
  Almond Chicken Kabobs, 20
  Chicken Stir-Fry, 86
  Fiesta Chicken Wings, 12
  Healthy Grilled Chicken Salad, 52
  Hot 'n' Spicy Chicken Barbecue, 58
  Sunshine Chicken Drumsticks, 14
  Tandoori-Style Chicken, 60
  Thai Chicken Ribbons, 22
Chili Marinade, 27
Citrus Grilled Steak, 40
Cowboy Kabobs, 12
Creamy Horseradish Sauce, 30
Curried Barbecue Sauce, 32
Curried Beef Pitas, 80

Fajita Kabobs, 79
Fiesta Chicken Wings, 12
**Fish**
  A.1. Grilled Fish Steaks, 38
  Fish in Foil, 58
  Lemon-Parsley Salmon Steaks, 46
**Fruit**
  Grilled Fruit Kabobs, 22
  Tangy Pineapple Fondue, 60
Fruit Glazed Beef Ribs, 80

Gazpacho Steak Roll, 36
Glazed Onion Sauce, 32
Greek Grilled Pizza Wedges, 18
Grilled Antipasto, 10
Grilled Beef 'n' Vegetable-Topped Pizza, 74
Grilled Fruit Kabobs, 22
Grilled Herbed Turkey Tenderloins, 50

Grilled Meat Loaf and Potatoes, 82
Grilled Sauerbraten Steak, 43
Grilled Steak and Asparagus Salad, 76
Grilled Steak and Pepper Sandwiches, 79
Grilled Steak au Poivre, 46
Grilled Steak with Blue Cheese Sauce, 44

Ham Steaks, Apricot-Glazed, 42
Healthy Grilled Chicken Salad, 52
Hearty Grilled Tenderloins, 40
Honey Basting Sauce, 26
Hot 'n' Spicy Chicken Barbecue, 58
Hot Blue Cheese Dip with Grilled Vegetables, 14

Indonesian Pork Chops 'n' Zesty Relish, 54

**Kabobs**
    Almond Chicken Kabobs, 20
    Asian Beef Bites, 16
    Beef and Bacon Shish Kabobs, 72
    Cowboy Kabobs, 12
    Fajita Kabobs, 79
    Grilled Fruit Kabobs, 22
    Hot Blue Cheese Dip with Grilled Vegetables, 14
    South-of-the-Border Vegetable Kabobs, 56
    Thai Chicken Ribbons, 22

Lamb, Barbecued Leg of, 56
Lemon-Parsley Salmon Steaks, 46
Lemon Pepper Marinade, 26

**Marinades** (*see also* **Bastes, Sauces**)
    Chili Marinade, 27
    Lemon Pepper Marinade, 26
    Steak Marinade Italiano, 28
    Steak Marinade Provençale, 27
    Tangy Marmalade Marinade, 32
    Teriyaki Marinade, 26
    Thai Marinade, 24
Mediterranean Burgers, 70
Mexican Flank Steak, 34
Mushroom Bacon Sauce, 28
Mushroom-Sauced Steak, 50

Onion Wine Sauce, 30
Orange Barbecue Sauce, 28

Pepper Trio Sauce, 24
Pesto Beef Swirls, 78
Philadelphia Cheese Steak Sandwiches, 90
**Pizza**
    Greek Grilled Pizza Wedges, 18
    Grilled Beef 'n' Vegetable-Topped Pizza, 74
**Pork**
    Barbecue Ribettes, 18
    Indonesian Pork Chops 'n' Zesty Relish, 54

Quick Barbecue Basting Sauce, 26

Raita, 60

**Salads**
    Grilled Steak and Asparagus Salad, 76
    Healthy Grilled Chicken Salad, 52
    Steak Ranchero, 48
    Wilted Steak Salad, 82
**Sandwiches**
    America's Favorite Cheddar Beef Burgers, 66
    Bacon Blue Burgers, 68

Beef 'n' Brie Sandwiches, 92
Big D Ranch Burgers, 62
Black Gold Burgers, 64
Blackened Burgers, 71
Burgers Canadian, 66
Burrito Burgers, 70
Curried Beef Pitas, 80
Grilled Steak and Pepper Sandwiches, 79
Mediterranean Burgers, 70
Philadelphia Cheese Steak Sandwiches, 90
Savory Stuffed Turkey Burgers, 68
Skillet Steak Fajitas, 84
Spicy Barbecue Beef Sandwich, 88
Super Cheeseburger, 71
Vegetarian Burgers, 64
**Sauces** (*see also* **Bastes, Marinades**)
    Bold Mushroom Sauce, 27
    Bold Pepper Sauce, 30
    Creamy Horseradish Sauce, 30
    Glazed Onion Sauce, 32
    Mushroom Bacon Sauce, 28
    Onion Wine Sauce, 30
    Pepper Trio Sauce, 24
    Raita, 60
Savory Grilled Tournedos, 44
Savory Onion Glazed Focaccia, 54
Savory Stuffed Turkey Burgers, 68
**Shellfish**
    Grilled Antipasto, 10
    Surf and Turf Brochettes, 16
Skillet Steak Fajitas, 84
South-of-the-Border Vegetable Kabobs, 56
Spicy Barbecue Beef Sandwich, 88
**Steak,** *see* **Beef**
Steak Diane, 92
Steak Marinade Italiano, 28
Steak Marinade Provençale, 27
Steak Ranchero, 48
Steak with Horseradish Sauce, 43
Stir-Fry Beef 'n' Broccoli, 90
Sunshine Chicken Drumsticks, 14
Super Cheeseburger, 71
Surf and Turf Brochettes, 16

Tandoori-Style Chicken, 60
Tangy Lemon Glaze, 27
Tangy Marmalade Marinade, 32
Tangy Pineapple Fondue, 60
Tenderloins with Roasted Garlic Sauce, 48
Teriyaki Marinade, 26
Teriyaki Steak Strips, 74
Thai Chicken Ribbons, 22
Thai Marinade, 24
30-Minute Chili Olé, 88
3-Star Hot Pepper Roulades, 76
Tijuana Blackened Steak, 36
Tournedos with Mushroom Wine Sauce, 42
**Turkey**
    Grilled Herbed Turkey Tenderloins, 50
    Hot Blue Cheese Dip with Grilled Vegetables, 14
    Savory Stuffed Turkey Burgers, 68

Vegetarian Burgers, 64

Wilted Steak Salad, 82

Zesty Lemon-Glazed Steak, 34